Pteranodon
ter - AN - oh - don

Triceratops
try - SER - a - tops

Tyrannosaurus rex
tie - RAN - oh - SAW - rus rex

Styracosaurus
sty - RAK - oh - SAW - rus

Tylosaurus
TIE - loh - SAW - rus

Brachiosaurus
BRAK - ee - oh - SAW - rus

Dunkleosteus
DUN - kl - OS - tee - us

Elasmosaurus
ee - LAZ - moh - SAW - rus

for aggs.

First Edition

ISBN 0-316-54584-8

Library of Congress Catalog Card Number 90-53340
Library of Congress Cataloging-in-Publication information is available.

10 9 8 7 6 5 4 3 2 1

Consultant: Dr Michael Benton,
University of Bristol

Created and produced by
David Bennett Books Ltd,
94 Victoria Street, St Albans,
Herts, AL1 3TG

Typesetting by Type City
Production by Imago
Printed in Hong Kong

IF DINOSAURS CAME TO TOWN

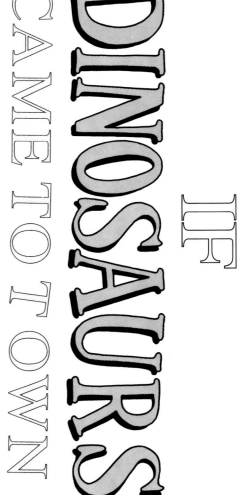

DOM MANSELL

Little, Brown and Company

Boston Toronto London

You probably know a bit about dinosaurs. They were prehistoric reptiles. Some of them were huge and some were tiny. Some were fierce and others were gentle.

They lived MILLIONS and MILLIONS and MILLIONS of years ago, long, long before there were buses or houses or even people.

Then they all died out. Nobody knows exactly why.

We know a lot about dinosaurs because scientists have found their bones, pieced them together again, and studied them VERY, VERY carefully.

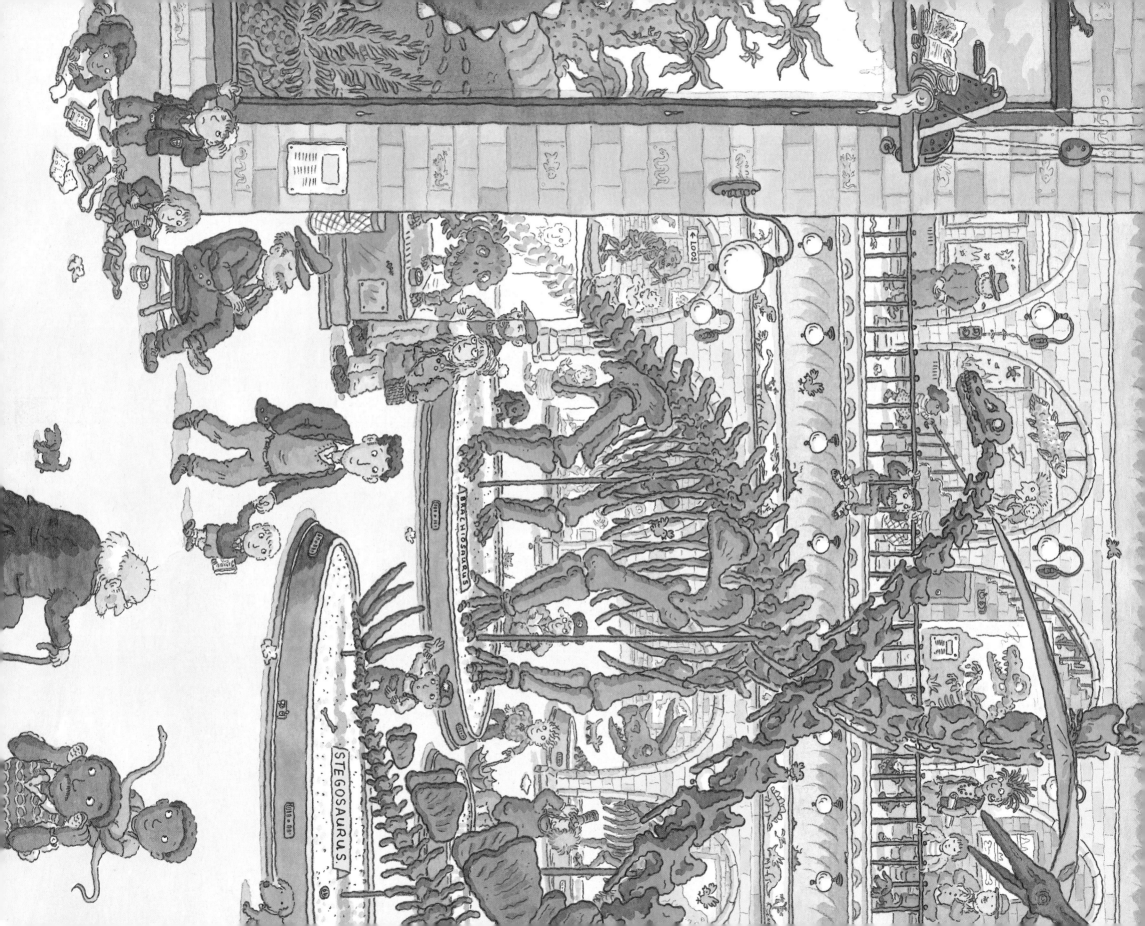

But can you imagine what these monsters were *really* like?
Well . . . just for a little while suppose that they hadn't all died.
Think what it would be like if a whole load of dinosaurs came
lumbering into your town . . .

These two have certainly jammed up
the traffic. That's not surprising when
you look at the size of them.
Diplodocus is the longest land animal
that's ever existed, and Brachiosaurus is the tallest.
But they're not at all fierce in spite of their size.

They have to MUNCH, MUNCH, MUNCH
all day long just to keep up their strength.
But don't worry. They eat only plants.
They wouldn't hurt you,
unless they stepped on you.
Then . . . SQUIDGE!
You'd be as flat as a pancake.

Not all dinosaurs are as gentle
as these two, though. . . .

SLICE! SLASH! GOBBLE! GUZZLE!

Beware of Deinonychus!

There's a whole gang of them down at the dump.

Deinonychus means "Terrible Claw,"

and that's what they've got — a huge, sharp, hooked

claw on each foot for RIPPING and SLITTING.

They're not very big, but they hunt in packs

and can bring down much bigger dinosaurs.

What's more, they can run faster than horses!

If they catch you, you've had it!

Allosaurus is fearsome enough

with his huge head and strong jaws,

but even *he* is keeping his distance

behind the steam shovel.

Maybe it will be safer

in the country.

Phew! That's better. Everything is quiet
and peaceful here.
Stegosaurus is having a big slurp of water,
and Ankylosaurus is quietly munching grass.
That's all they eat — grass and other plants.

Stegosaurus has big, bony plates along her back.
The wind blows over them and helps to keep
her cool. If you disturb her, she will wave
her spiky tail around, so be careful.

Ankylosaurus is hard and knobbly all over.
If another dinosaur tried to bite him,
it would break its teeth! He uses that club
on the end of his tail to whack his enemies,
so that ram had better watch out!

Things aren't quite so peaceful out at sea.
Two hungry sea reptiles, Elasmosaurus and
Tylosaurus, are after the fishermen.

Elasmosaurus has four strong flippers
that zoom him through the sea.
He can lift his head right out of the water,
to snap at you with his needle-sharp teeth!

Tylosaurus is like a huge crocodile with flippers.
She swishes her strong tail from side to side
to push herself through the water.
Look at the size of her mouth!
She'd chew you into mincemeat
in no time with those giant teeth.
(She's got more than seventy of them.)

Quick! Dive for cover!
SPLOOSH!

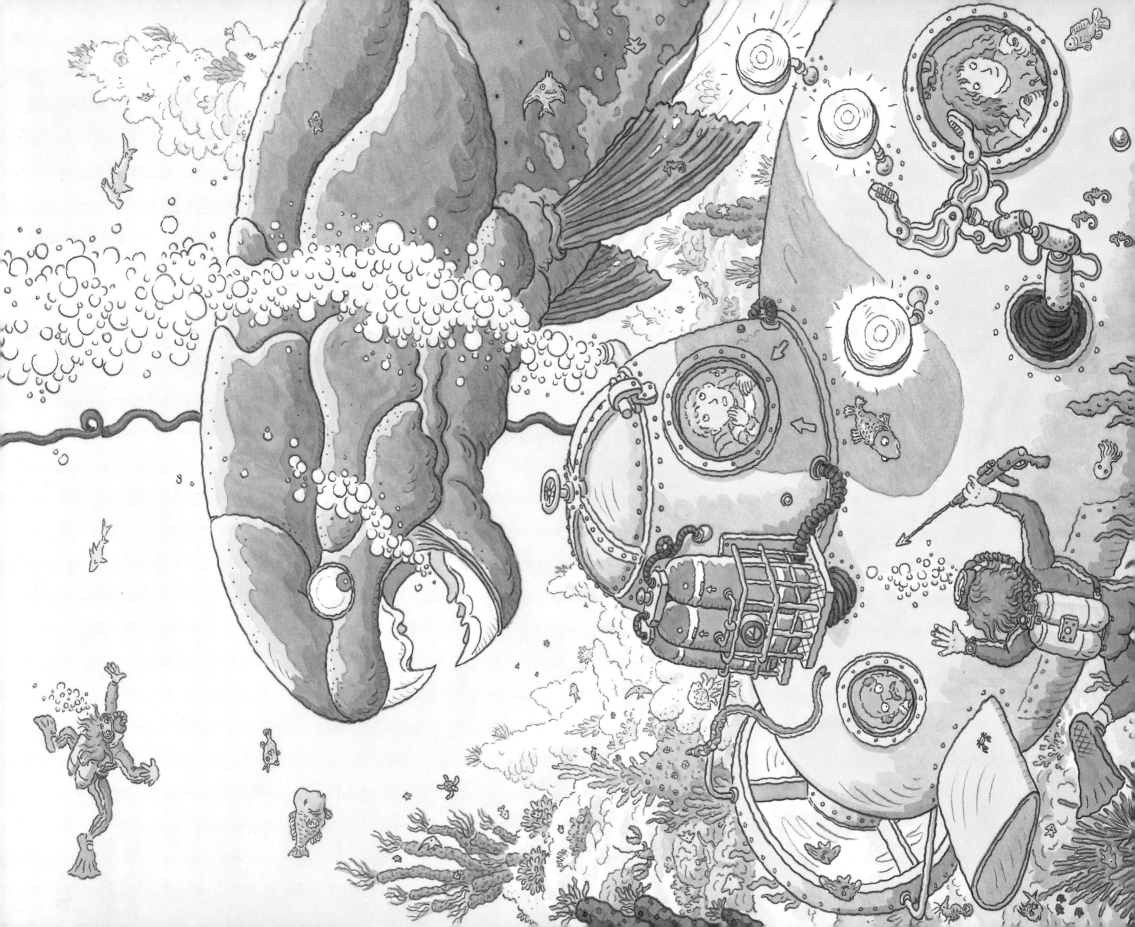

Oh, no! Things are even worse down here!
Rushing through the water comes Dunkleosteus.
He's a gigantic prehistoric fish — a nightmare with fins.
He's got a huge, armored head with strong jaws
of sharpened bone. He crunches open
the stone-hard fish he likes to eat — CRACK!
But *you* might make a JUICIER meal,
so let's get out of here. Hurry!

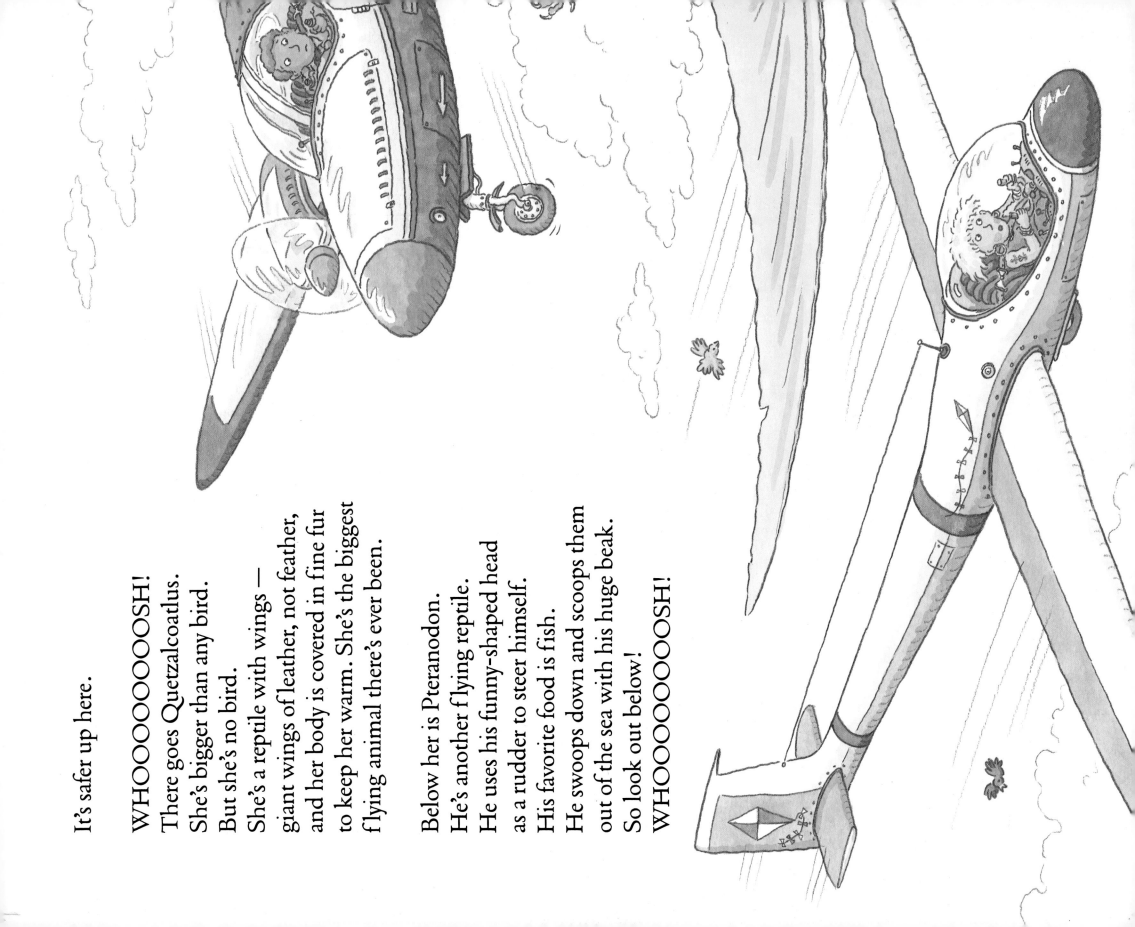

It's safer up here.

WHOOOOOOSH!
There goes Quetzalcoatlus.
She's bigger than any bird.
But she's no bird.
She's a reptile with wings —
giant wings of leather, not feather,
and her body is covered in fine fur
to keep her warm. She's the biggest
flying animal there's ever been.

Below her is Pteranodon.
He's another flying reptile.
He uses his funny-shaped head
as a rudder to steer himself.
His favorite food is fish.
He swoops down and scoops them
out of the sea with his huge beak.
So look out below!
WHOOOOOOOSH!

This is Dimorphodon.
He's like a big bat.
Isn't he creepy?

Back in town, there's trouble on High Street. Triceratops and Styracosaurus are about to charge the security van! They don't want the money, though. They think it's another dinosaur, and they want to frighten it off.

Triceratops is like a huge rhinoceros. Her skin is tough, her legs are strong, and just look at those horns! "Three-Horn-Face." That's what her name means.

Styracosaurus means "Spike-Lizard." You can see why. His bony frill protects his neck from other dinosaurs' teeth. The strong muscles there help his beak snap off the tough shrubs he likes to eat.

BANK

You may think you'd be safe from dinosaurs at home, but oh, no! There are plenty of prehistoric animals small enough to get into your bedroom. Look at them all!

Bagaceratops is on the bed, protecting her newly hatched babies. Diplocaulus has taken over the fish tank. His boomerang-shaped head helps him shoot through the water.

Oops! Don't step on Ophiderpeton! He's asleep under the carpet. He looks like a snake — but actually he's an amphibian. So is Eryops (he's the one snoozing in the bathtub).

Over by the window is feathery Avimimus. If you didn't know any better, you might think she was a bird. What's that she's looking at? AAAAGH!

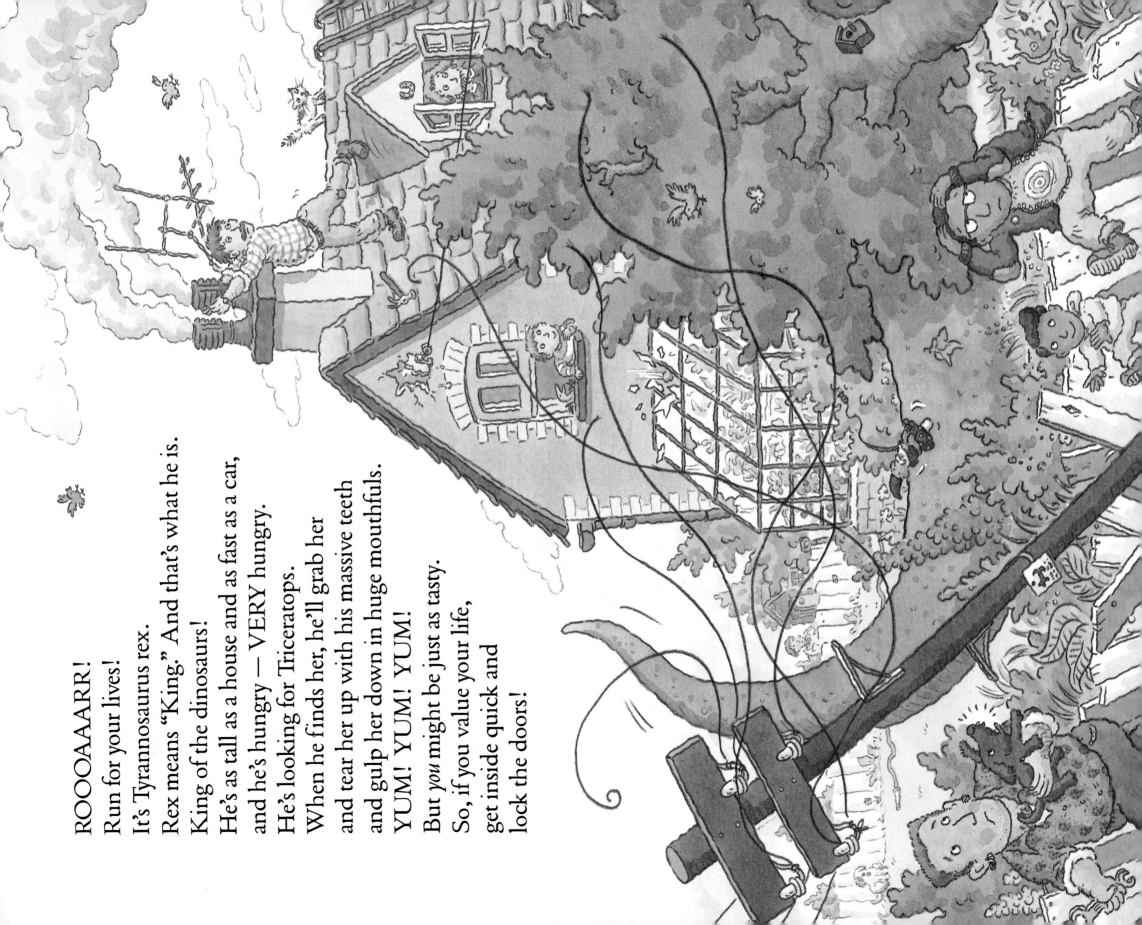

ROOOAAARR!
Run for your lives!
It's Tyrannosaurus rex.
Rex means "King." And that's what he is.
King of the dinosaurs!
He's as tall as a house and as fast as a car,
and he's hungry — VERY hungry.
He's looking for Triceratops.
When he finds her, he'll grab her
and tear her up with his massive teeth
and gulp her down in huge mouthfuls.
YUM! YUM! YUM!
But *you* might be just as tasty.
So, if you value your life,
get inside quick and
lock the doors!

WOW! If only dinosaurs could *really* come back!
It would be FANTASTIC. . . .
or would it? What do you think?

Here are some more dinosaurs and prehistoric reptiles — can you imagine what it would be like if *they* came to town?

Rhamphorhynchus
RAM - for - RINK - us

Struthiomimus
STROOTH - ee - oh - MIME - us

Dimetrodon
die - MEET - roh - don

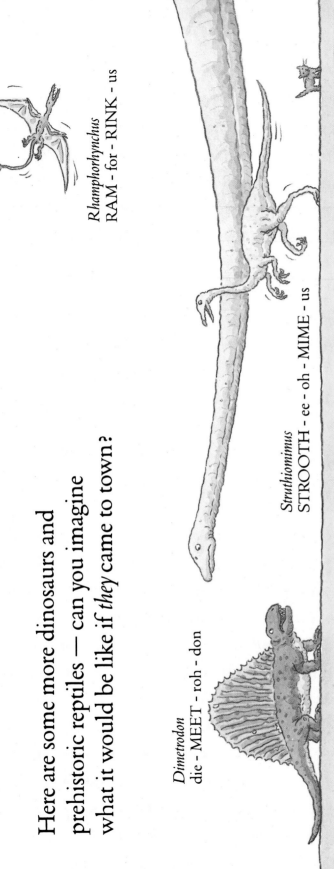

Spinosaurus
SPINE - o - SAW - rus

Kentrosaurus
KEN - tro - SAW - rus

Torosaurus
TOR - o - SAW - rus

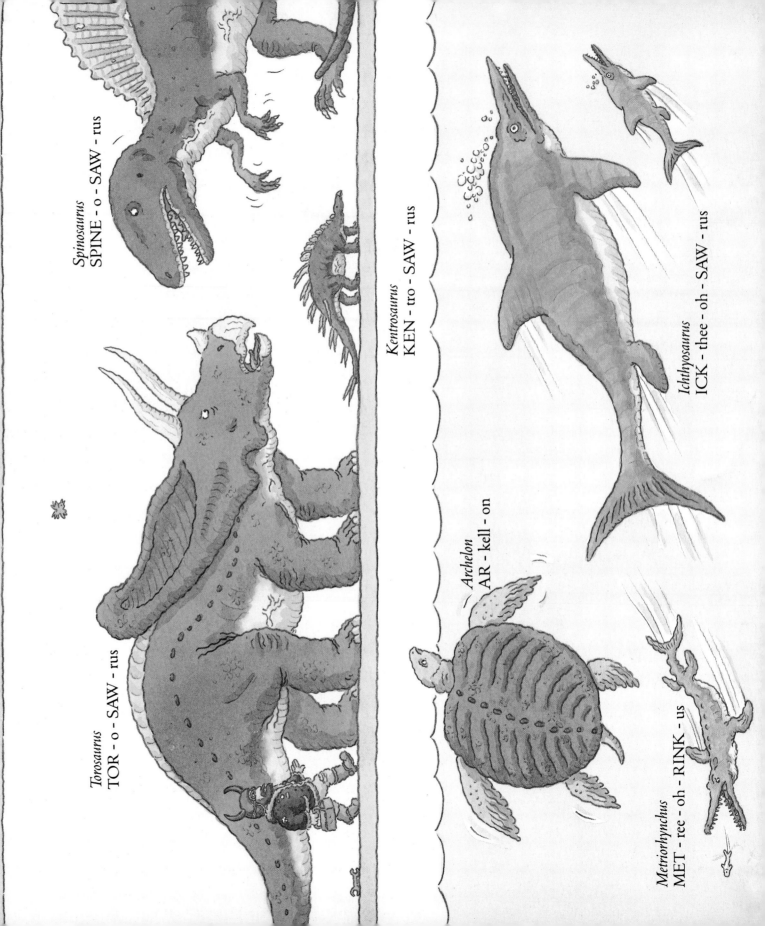

Ichthyosaurus
ICK - thee - oh - SAW - rus

Archelon
AR - kell - on

Metriorhynchus
MET - ree - oh - RINK - us